contents

the wok	2
seafood	4
chicken	10
beef	18
lamb	30
pork	40
vegetarian	50
glossary	60
conversion chart	62
index	63

NZ, Canada, US and UK readers
Please note that Australian spoon and cup measurements are metric.
A conversion chart appears on page 62.

THE

What could be easier than meat, vegies and a wok? Stir-frying is the perfect way to help you get the recommended five servings of vegetables a day, and it's a quick dinner fix for any night of the week.

Although a heavy-based frying pan will do the job, a wok is the perfect shape for cooking stir-fries. A new wok needs to be seasoned before its first use. This will enhance the flavour of food cooked in it, and will also create a smooth surface that food is less likely to stick to. Stainless steel and non-stick woks do not need seasoning. Clean your new wok thoroughly with warm, soapy water and a scrubbing brush then, in a well-ventilated kitchen, heat the wok until the entire surface is hot. Use a piece of cloth or a heatproof brush to apply a thin layer of cooking oil over the entire inner

WOK

surface of the wok. (Use an oil with a high smoking point, such as peanut oil, to minimise oil fumes. Polyunsaturated oils are not recommended as they can make the wok sticky.) Burn the oil into the wok by tilting the wok from side to side. Ensure every part of the surface is given direct heat from the stove. Let the pan cool completely to room temperature, then wipe out excess oil with a paper towel. Repeat two to five times until the wok begins to turn dark. It should have an oily surface that does not look dry when heated. Your wok is then ready for cooking.

Ensure all your ingredients are chopped and marinated (if required) prior to cooking. Pieces should be of even size so that they are cooked consistently. Have everything ready and at hand, including any sauces,

nuts or noodles, because once you start, you'll have no time to peel onions or chop the vegetables. Heat the wok before adding any oil, and make sure the oil is hot prior to adding the food.

Cook the meat first, in batches, so the pan is not overcrowded and the meat doesn't stew. Add a little more oil and any aromatic ingredients such as garlic or chilli next. Vegetables should be added so the harder ones, such as onion and baby corn, are given the longest time to cook, and the softest vegetables, such as mushrooms and leafy greens, are only cooked briefly. Return meat to the wok with any sauces, nuts and noodles; stir-fry until heated through. After use, just wash in warm soapy water (don't use abrasives) – and dry well. If food starts to stick to the wok, season it again.

chilli crab

8 uncooked large blue swimmer crabs (2.5kg)
1 tablespoon peanut oil
4 fresh small red thai chillies, chopped finely
8cm piece fresh ginger (40g), grated
4 cloves garlic, crushed
1 tablespoon fish sauce
⅓ cup (80ml) tomato sauce
¼ cup (60ml) sweet chilli sauce
2 tablespoons brown sugar
1 cup (250ml) fish stock
1 cup (250ml) water
¼ cup coarsely chopped fresh coriander

1   Remove v-shaped flaps on the undersides of crabs. Turn crabs over and place a knife in the seam between back two legs; push up to lever off the shells. Pull the shells up and off.

2   Remove and discard gills. Cut each crab in half through the centre of the body; remove and discard liver and brain matter; rinse lightly (avoid using too much water for this and don't rinse under a running tap – as doing so will dilute the delicate flavour).

3   Remove claws; crack both claw sections using a shellfish cracker, a nutcracker or a meat mallet – this allows the spicy sauce to be absorbed and makes it easier to remove the flesh for eating.

4   Heat oil in wok; cook chilli, ginger and garlic until fragrant. Add combined sauces, then sugar, stock and the water; stir until mixture boils. Transfer two-thirds of the sauce to a jug; reserve.

5   Add claws to wok; stir-fry about 4 minutes or until claws have changed in colour and are just cooked through. Remove claws from wok; cover to keep warm. Add half the reserved sauce and half the crab bodies to wok; stir-fry 5 minutes or until cooked through, remove. Repeat with remaining sauce and crab bodies. Serve sprinkled with coriander.

serves 4
preparation time 20 minutes
cooking time 15 minutes
nutritional count per serving 6.2g total fat (1.1g saturated fat); 932kJ (223 cal); 18.8 carbohydrate; 21.6g protein; 2.1g fibre

kung pao prawns

Kung pao, a classic Sichuan stir-fry, is made with either seafood or chicken, peanuts and lots of chillies. An authentic Sichuan-Chinese restaurant always has a delicious kung pao.

28 uncooked large king prawns (2kg)
2 tablespoons peanut oil
2 cloves garlic, crushed
4 fresh small red thai chillies, chopped finely
1 teaspoon sichuan peppercorns, crushed
500g choy sum, trimmed, chopped coarsely
¼ cup (60ml) light soy sauce
¼ cup (60ml) chinese cooking wine
1 teaspoon white sugar
227g can water chestnuts, rinsed, halved
4 green onions, chopped coarsely
½ cup (70g) roasted unsalted peanuts

1   Shell and devein prawns, leaving tails intact.
2   Heat half the oil in wok; stir-fry prawns, in batches, until changed in colour.
3   Heat remaining oil in wok; stir-fry garlic, chilli and peppercorns until fragrant. Add choy sum; stir-fry until wilted. Return prawns to wok with sauce, wine, sugar and chestnuts; stir-fry 2 minutes. Remove from heat; stir in onion and nuts.

serves 4
preparation time 30 minutes
cooking time 15 minutes
nutritional count per serving 19.4g total fat (2.9g saturated fat); 1998kJ (478 cal); 8.5g carbohydrate; 8.5g protein; 7.5g fibre

salt and pepper squid with cucumber salad

500g cleaned squid hoods
½ teaspoon cracked
    black pepper
1 teaspoon sea salt
½ teaspoon lemon pepper
    seasoning
1 tablespoon peanut oil
cucumber salad
1 lebanese cucumber (130g),
    sliced thinly
2 green onions, sliced thinly
250g cherry tomatoes, halved
⅓ cup (50g) roasted unsalted
    peanuts, chopped coarsely
½ cup loosely packed
    fresh mint leaves
1 tablespoon red wine vinegar
1 tablespoon peanut oil

1 Cut squid hoods along one side and open out. Using a small sharp knife, score inside of hoods in a diagonal pattern, without cutting all the way through (this will allow the squid to curl during cooking). Cut each squid hood into eight pieces.
2 Make cucumber salad.
3 Sprinkle squid with combined pepper, salt and lemon pepper seasoning.
4 Heat oil in wok; stir-fry squid, in batches, until curled and just cooked through. Serve squid with cucumber salad.
cucumber salad Combine cucumber, onion, tomato, nuts and mint in medium bowl. Add combined vinegar and oil; toss gently.

serves 4
preparation time 20 minutes
cooking time 10 minutes
nutritional count per serving 16.7g total fat (2.8g saturated fat); 1124kJ (269 cal); 3.7g carbohydrate; 24.8g protein; 3g fibre

chicken and thai basil stir-fry

2 tablespoons peanut oil
600g chicken breast fillets, sliced thinly
2 cloves garlic, crushed
1cm piece fresh ginger (5g), grated
4 fresh small red thai chillies, sliced thinly
4 fresh kaffir lime leaves, shredded finely
1 medium brown onion (150g), sliced thinly
100g mushrooms, quartered
1 large carrot (180g), sliced thinly
¼ cup (60ml) oyster sauce
1 tablespoon soy sauce
1 tablespoon fish sauce
⅓ cup (80ml) chicken stock
1 cup (80g) bean sprouts
¾ cup loosely packed thai basil leaves

1 Heat half the oil in wok; stir-fry chicken, in batches, until browned all over and cooked through.
2 Heat remaining oil in wok; stir-fry garlic, ginger, chilli, lime leaves and onion until onion softens and mixture is fragrant. Add mushrooms and carrot; stir-fry until carrot is just tender. Return chicken to wok with sauces and stock; stir-fry until sauce thickens slightly. Remove from heat; stir through sprouts and basil.

serves 4
preparation time 20 minutes
cooking time 15 minutes
nutritional count per serving 15.9g total fat (3.5g saturated fat); 1367kJ (327 cal); 9.2g carbohydrate; 35g protein; 3.4g fibre

pad sieu

1kg fresh wide rice noodles
2 teaspoons sesame oil
2 cloves garlic, crushed
2 fresh small red thai chillies, sliced thinly
600g chicken thigh fillets, chopped coarsely
250g baby buk choy, quartered lengthways
4 green onions, sliced thinly
2 tablespoons kecap manis
1 tablespoon oyster sauce
1 tablespoon fish sauce
1 tablespoon grated palm sugar
¼ cup coarsely chopped fresh coriander
1 tablespoon fried shallots

1 Place noodles in large heatproof bowl, cover with boiling water; separate with fork, drain.

2 Heat oil in wok; stir-fry garlic and chilli until fragrant. Add chicken; stir-fry until browned lightly. Add buk choy and onion; stir-fry until onion softens and chicken is cooked through.

3 Add noodles with kecap manis, sauces and sugar; stir-fry, tossing gently to combine. Remove from heat; add coriander, tossing gently to combine. Sprinkle with fried shallots.

serves 4
preparation time 15 minutes
cooking time 15 minutes
nutritional count per serving 14.4g total fat (3.7g saturated fat); 2165kJ (518 cal); 59.9g carbohydrate; 35.1g protein; 2.7g fibre
tip Fried shallots provide an extra crunchy finish to a salad, stir-fry or curry. They can be purchased at all Asian grocery stores; once opened, they will keep for months if stored in a tightly sealed glass jar. Make your own by frying thinly sliced peeled shallots until golden brown and crisp.

chicken fried rice

You need to cook 2 cups (400g) of white long-grain rice the day before making this recipe. Spread evenly onto a tray; refrigerate overnight.

1 tablespoon vegetable oil
2 eggs, beaten lightly
3 rindless bacon rashers (195g), chopped coarsely
2 cloves garlic, crushed
2cm piece fresh ginger (10g), grated
1½ cups (240g) coarsely chopped cooked chicken
4 cups cold cooked rice
1 cup (120g) frozen pea and corn mixture
¼ cup (60ml) light soy sauce
1 cup (80g) bean sprouts
6 green onions, sliced thinly

1 Heat half the oil in wok; cook egg over medium heat, swirling wok to form thin omelette. Remove from wok; cool. Roll omelette tightly; cut into thin strips.
2 Heat remaining oil in wok; stir-fry bacon, garlic and ginger until bacon is crisp.
3 Add chicken; stir-fry 1 minute. Add rice, frozen vegetables and sauce; stir-fry until hot. Add sprouts, onion and omelette; stir-fry 1 minute.

serves 4
preparation time 10 minutes
cooking time 15 minutes
nutritional count per serving 21.9g total fat (5.9g saturated fat); 2362kJ (565 cal); 52.6g carbohydrate; 37.2g protein; 3.8g fibre
tip You can purchase half a barbecued chicken or use any leftover cooked chicken for this recipe.

singapore noodles

You need to purchase a large barbecued chicken weighing approximately 900g to get the amount of shredded meat needed for this recipe.

450g singapore noodles
1 teaspoon peanut oil
1 small brown onion (80g), sliced finely
2 rindless bacon rashers (130g), chopped finely
3cm piece fresh ginger (15g), grated
1 tablespoon mild curry powder
3 cups (480g) shredded barbecued chicken
6 green onions, sliced thinly
1½ tablespoons light soy sauce
⅓ cup (80ml) sweet sherry

1 Place noodles in large heatproof bowl, cover with boiling water; separate with fork, drain.
2 Heat oil in wok, add brown onion, bacon and ginger; stir-fry about 2 minutes or until onion softens and bacon is crisp. Add curry powder; stir-fry until fragrant.
3 Add noodles and remaining ingredients; stir-fry until hot.

serves 4
preparation time 15 minutes
cooking time 10 minutes
nutritional count per serving 15.5g total fat (4.6g saturated fat); 1944kJ (465 cal); 32.7g carbohydrate; 41.9g protein; 3.2g fibre

mee goreng

Mee goreng, from Indonesia and Malaysia, simply translates as fried noodles, and is an everyday dish in that part of the world. Beef strips can be prepared from blade, fillet, rib-eye, round, rump, sirloin or topside steak.

600g hokkien noodles
1 tablespoon peanut oil
3 eggs, beaten lightly
500g beef strips
2 cloves garlic, crushed
2cm piece fresh ginger (10g), grated
500g baby buk choy, chopped coarsely
¼ cup coarsely chopped fresh coriander
4 green onions, sliced thinly
2 tablespoons dried shrimp
¼ cup (60ml) kecap manis
2 teaspoons sambal oelek
¼ cup (60ml) beef stock
½ cup (70g) roasted unsalted peanuts, chopped coarsely

1 Place noodles in large heatproof bowl, cover with boiling water; separate with fork, drain.
2 Heat 1 teaspoon of the oil in wok; add half the egg, swirl wok to make thin omelette. Cook, uncovered, until egg is just set. Remove omelette from wok; repeat with a further 1 teaspoon of the oil and remaining egg. Roll omelettes tightly; slice thinly.
3 Heat remaining oil in wok; stir-fry combined beef, garlic and ginger, in batches, until beef is browned all over and just cooked through.
4 Add buk choy to wok; stir-fry until just wilted. Return beef to pan with noodles, coriander, onion, shrimp and combined kecap manis, sambal and stock; stir-fry until heated through. Serve topped with omelette and peanuts.

serves 4
preparation time 10 minutes
cooking time 15 minutes
nutritional count per serving 31.1g total fat (8.6g saturated fat); 3507kJ (839 cal); 82.3g carbohydrate; 53.5g protein; 6.6g fibre

beef with oyster sauce

400g buk choy
250g gai lan
2 tablespoons peanut oil
2 cloves garlic, crushed
500g beef rump steak, sliced thinly
50g snow peas
425g can baby corn, rinsed, drained
6 green onions, chopped coarsely
2 tablespoons oyster sauce
1 tablespoon fish sauce
1 tablespoon brown sugar

1 Break buk choy and gai lan into large pieces; boil, steam or microwave until just tender, drain well. Cover to keep warm.

2 Heat oil in wok; stir-fry garlic and beef, in batches, until beef is browned and just cooked.

3 Add peas, corn, onion, sauces and sugar to wok; stir-fry until peas are almost tender.

4 Return beef to wok; stir-fry about 2 minutes or until heated through. Serve mixture over buk choy and gai lan.

serves 4
preparation time 15 minutes
cooking time 10 minutes
nutritional count per serving 18.1g total fat (5.4g saturated fat); 1463kJ (350 cal); 10.6g carbohydrate; 33g protein; 6.7g fibre

ginger teriyaki beef

⅓ cup (80ml) teriyaki sauce
½ cup (125ml) hoisin sauce
2 tablespoons mirin
1 tablespoon peanut oil
750g beef strips
250g broccoli, cut into florets
250g sugar snap peas, trimmed
115g baby corn, halved lengthways
4cm piece fresh ginger (20g), grated
1½ cups (120g) bean sprouts

1 Combine sauces and mirin in small jug.
2 Heat half the oil in wok; stir-fry beef, in batches, until browned.
3 Heat remaining oil in wok; stir-fry broccoli until almost tender.
4 Return beef to wok with sauce mixture, peas, corn and ginger. Stir-fry until vegetables and beef are cooked. Remove from heat; sprinkle with sprouts.

serves 4
preparation time 10 minutes
cooking time 15 minutes
nutritional count per serving 20.7g total fat (7.2g saturated fat); 2073kJ (496 cal); 23.2g carbohydrate; 48g protein; 10.5g fibre

beef in satay sauce

1 tablespoon peanut oil
750g beef strips
1 fresh long red chilli, sliced thinly
1 medium brown onion (150g), sliced thinly
1 medium red capsicum (200g), sliced thinly
½ cup (140g) crunchy peanut butter
½ cup (125ml) coconut cream
¼ cup (60ml) sweet chilli sauce
1 tablespoon japanese soy sauce

1 Heat half the oil in wok; stir-fry beef, in batches, until cooked.
2 Heat remaining oil in wok; stir-fry chilli, onion and capsicum until soft; remove from wok.
3 Combine peanut butter, coconut cream and sauces in wok; bring to a boil. Return beef and onion mixture to wok; stir-fry until hot.

serves 4
preparation time 10 minutes
cooking time 20 minutes
nutritional count per serving 42.2g total fat (15g saturated fat); 2629kJ (629 cal); 10.6g carbohydrate; 49.8g protein; 6.1g fibre

hokkien mee with beef

450g hokkien noodles
1 tablespoon peanut oil
600g piece eye fillet, sliced thinly
1 medium brown onion (150g), sliced thinly
2 cloves garlic, crushed
1 medium red capsicum (200g), sliced thinly
115g baby corn, halved lengthways
150g snow peas, trimmed, halved diagonally
2 baby buk choy (300g), chopped coarsely
¼ cup (95g) char siu sauce
1 tablespoon dark soy sauce
¼ cup (60ml) chicken stock

1 Place noodles in medium heatproof bowl, cover with boiling water; separate with fork, drain.
2 Heat half the oil in wok; stir-fry beef, in batches, until browned.
3 Heat remaining oil in wok; stir-fry onion, garlic and capsicum until tender.
4 Return beef to wok with noodles, corn, snow peas, buk choy, sauces and stock; stir-fry until vegetables are tender and beef is cooked as desired.

serves 4
preparation time 15 minutes
cooking time 15 minutes
nutritional count per serving 32.3g total fat (13.8g saturated fat); 3382kJ (809 cal); 75.5g carbohydrate; 47.1g protein; 13.3g fibre
tip Hokkien, also known as stir-fry noodles, are fresh chinese wheat noodles that resemble thick, yellow-brown spaghetti.

beef chow mein

1 tablespoon vegetable oil
500g beef mince
1 medium brown onion (150g), chopped finely
2 cloves garlic, crushed
1 tablespoon curry powder
1 large carrot (180g), chopped finely
2 trimmed celery stalks (200g), sliced thinly
150g mushrooms, sliced thinly
1 cup (250ml) chicken stock
⅓ cup (80ml) oyster sauce
2 tablespoons dark soy sauce
440g thin fresh egg noodles
½ cup (60g) frozen peas
½ small wombok (350g), shredded coarsely

1 Heat oil in wok; stir-fry beef, onion and garlic until beef is browned. Add curry powder; stir-fry 1 minute or until fragrant. Add carrot, celery and mushrooms; stir-fry until vegetables soften.
2 Add stock, sauces and noodles; stir-fry 2 minutes. Add peas and wombok; stir-fry until wombok just wilts.

serves 4
preparation time 20 minutes
cooking time 20 minutes
nutritional count per serving 15.7g total fat (4.6g saturated fat); 2571kJ (615 cal); 70.6g carbohydrate; 42.3g protein; 8.4g fibre

mongolian lamb stir-fry

1½ cups (300g) white long-grain rice
2 tablespoons peanut oil
600g lamb strips
2 cloves garlic, crushed
1cm piece fresh ginger (5g), grated
1 medium brown onion (150g), sliced thickly
1 medium red capsicum (200g), sliced thickly
230g can bamboo shoots, rinsed, drained
¼ cup (60ml) japanese soy sauce
1 tablespoon black bean sauce
1 tablespoon cornflour
2 tablespoons rice wine vinegar
6 green onions, cut into 5cm lengths

1 Cook rice in large saucepan of boiling water, uncovered, until just tender; drain. Cover to keep warm.
2 Meanwhile, heat half the oil in wok; stir-fry lamb, in batches, until browned all over.
3 Heat remaining oil in wok; stir-fry garlic, ginger and brown onion until onion softens. Add capsicum and bamboo shoots; stir-fry until vegetables are just tender. Return lamb to wok with sauces and blended cornflour and vinegar; stir-fry until sauce boils and thickens slightly. Remove from heat; stir in green onion. Serve stir-fry with rice.

serves 4
preparation time 15 minutes
cooking time 20 minutes
nutritional count per serving 23.2g total fat (7.8g saturated fat); 2709kJ (648 cal); 68.7g carbohydrate; 40.4g protein; 3.5g fibre

larb lamb

1 tablespoon peanut oil
5cm stick fresh lemon grass
  (10g), chopped finely
2 fresh small red thai chillies,
  chopped finely
2 cloves garlic, crushed
3cm piece fresh ginger (15g),
  chopped finely
750g lamb mince
1 lebanese cucumber (130g),
  seeded, sliced thinly
1 small red onion (100g),
  sliced thinly
1 cup (80g) bean sprouts
½ cup loosely packed thai
  basil leaves
1 cup loosely packed fresh
  coriander leaves
8 large iceberg lettuce leaves
larb dressing
⅓ cup (80ml) lime juice
2 tablespoons fish sauce
2 tablespoons kecap manis
2 tablespoons peanut oil
2 teaspoons grated
  palm sugar
½ teaspoon sambal oelek

1 Make larb dressing.
2 Heat oil in wok; stir-fry lemon grass, chilli, garlic and ginger until fragrant.
3 Add lamb; stir-fry until changed in colour.
4 Add a third of the dressing to mixture in wok; stir-fry about 2 minutes or until most of the liquid has evaporated.
5 Place remaining dressing in large bowl; add lamb mixture, cucumber, onion, sprouts and herbs; toss larb to combine. Serve larb in lettuce leaves.

larb dressing Combine ingredients in screw-top jar; shake well.

serves 4
preparation time 20 minutes
cooking time 15 minutes
nutritional count per serving 26.9g total fat (8.3g saturated fat); 1852kJ (443 cal); 6.1g carbohydrate; 42.1g protein; 3.7g fibre

crisp twice-fried lamb with thai basil

⅓ cup (80ml) sweet chilli sauce
¼ cup (60ml) oyster sauce
2 tablespoons light soy sauce
800g lamb strips
¾ cup (110g) plain flour
vegetable oil, for deep-frying
1 tablespoon vegetable oil, extra
1 small brown onion (80g), sliced thinly
2 cloves garlic, sliced thinly
250g sugar snap peas, trimmed
2 cups (160g) bean sprouts
1 cup loosely packed thai basil leaves

1 Combine sauces in small jug; pour two-thirds of the sauce mixture into medium bowl with lamb, mix well. Drain lamb, discard liquid.
2 Coat lamb in flour; shake off excess. Heat oil in wok; deep-fry lamb, in batches, until browned, drain. (Cool oil; remove from wok and reserve for another use.)
3 Heat extra oil in cleaned wok; stir-fry onion and garlic until onion softens. Add peas and remaining sauce mixture; stir-fry until peas are almost tender.
4 Return lamb to wok; stir-fry until hot. Remove from heat; stir in sprouts and basil.

serves 4
preparation time 15 minutes
cooking time 20 minutes
nutritional count per serving 34.5g total fat (10.2g saturated fat); 2713kJ (649 cal); 32.4g carbohydrate; 49.6g protein; 5.4g fibre

char siu lamb and noodle stir-fry

2 cloves garlic, crushed
2cm piece fresh ginger (10g), grated
1 tablespoon finely grated orange rind
1 teaspoon sesame oil
750g lamb strips
450g hokkien noodles
2 tablespoons peanut oil
200g sugar snap peas
115g baby corn, halved lengthways
2 fresh long red chillies, sliced thinly
⅓ cup (120g) char siu sauce
2 tablespoons water
1 tablespoon rice wine vinegar

1 Combine garlic, ginger, rind, sesame oil and lamb in medium bowl.
2 Place noodles in large heatproof bowl, cover with boiling water; separate with fork, drain.
3 Heat half the peanut oil in wok; stir-fry peas and corn until just tender. Remove from wok.
4 Heat remaining peanut oil in wok; stir-fry lamb, in batches, until browned all over and cooked as desired. Return peas, corn and lamb to wok with noodles, chilli and combined sauce, water and vinegar; stir-fry until heated through.

serves 4
preparation time 15 minutes
cooking time 20 minutes
nutritional count per serving 29.2g total fat (9.6g saturated fat); 2725kJ (652 cal); 46.6g carbohydrate; 47.1g protein; 8g fibre

honey and five-spice lamb with buk choy

¼ teaspoon five-spice powder
¼ cup (60ml) oyster sauce
2 tablespoons honey
2 tablespoons rice vinegar
2 cloves garlic, crushed
600g lamb fillets, sliced thinly
400g fresh thin rice noodles
1 tablespoon sesame oil
2 fresh long red chillies, sliced thinly
2cm piece fresh ginger (10g), cut into matchsticks
1 medium red onion (170g), sliced thickly
500g baby buk choy, leaves separated
¼ cup firmly packed fresh coriander leaves
1 tablespoon crushed peanuts

1 Combine five-spice, sauce, honey, vinegar and garlic in small bowl.
2 Combine lamb with 1 tablespoon of the five-spice mixture in medium bowl.
3 Place noodles in large heatproof bowl, cover with boiling water; separate noodles with fork, drain.
4 Heat oil in wok; stir-fry lamb, in batches, until browned all over. Return to wok; add remaining five-spice mixture, chilli, ginger and onion; stir-fry until onion softens. Add noodles and buk choy; stir-fry until hot.
5 Serve stir-fry sprinkled with coriander and nuts.

serves 4
preparation time 15 minutes
cooking time 10 minutes
nutritional count per serving 12.2g total fat (3.3g saturated fat); 1781kJ (426 cal); 40.7g carbohydrate; 36.1g protein; 3.3g fibre

pork and chicken sang choy bow

500g pork fillets
⅓ cup (120g) char siu sauce
1 tablespoon peanut oil
150g chicken mince
1 clove garlic, crushed
100g fresh shiitake mushrooms, chopped finely
190g can water chestnuts, rinsed, drained, chopped finely
2 green onions, chopped finely
2 tablespoons oyster sauce
1 tablespoon soy sauce
1 teaspoon sesame oil
1½ cups (120g) bean sprouts
8 large iceberg lettuce leaves
2 green onions, sliced thinly

1 Preheat oven to 180°C/160°C fan-forced.
2 Place pork on wire rack in large shallow baking dish; brush all over with ¼ cup of the char siu sauce. Roast, uncovered, about 40 minutes or until cooked through, brushing occasionally with pan drippings. Cool 10 minutes; chop pork finely.
3 Meanwhile, heat peanut oil in wok; stir-fry chicken, garlic and mushrooms, 5 minutes. Add water chestnuts, chopped onion, oyster sauce, soy sauce, sesame oil, pork and remaining char siu sauce; stir-fry until chicken is cooked through. Remove from heat; add sprouts, toss gently to combine.
4 Divide lettuce leaves among serving plates; spoon mixture into leaves, sprinkle each with sliced onion.

serves 4
preparation time 20 minutes
cooking time 45 minutes
nutritional count per serving 13.4g total fat (3.1g saturated fat); 1430kJ (342 cal); 17.5g carbohydrate; 37.9g protein; 6.1g fibre

mee krob

150g fresh silken firm tofu
vegetable oil, for deep-frying
125g rice vermicelli
2 tablespoons peanut oil
2 eggs, beaten lightly
1 tablespoon water
2 cloves garlic, crushed
2 fresh small red thai chillies,
    chopped finely
1 small green thai chilli,
    chopped finely
2 tablespoons grated
    palm sugar
2 tablespoons fish sauce
2 tablespoons tomato sauce
1 tablespoon rice wine vinegar
200g pork mince
200g shelled cooked small
    prawns, chopped coarsely
6 green onions, sliced thinly
¼ cup firmly packed fresh
    coriander leaves

1 Pat tofu with absorbent paper, cut into slices; cut slices into 1cm-wide matchsticks. Spread on tray lined with absorbent paper; cover with more absorbent paper, stand 10 minutes.

2 Heat vegetable oil in wok; deep-fry vermicelli, in batches, until puffed. Drain.

3 Deep-fry tofu, in batches, until browned lightly. Drain on absorbent paper.

4 Heat 2 teaspoons of the peanut oil in cleaned wok; add half the combined egg and water, swirl wok to make thin omelette. Cook, uncovered, until egg is just set. Remove from wok; roll omelette then cut into thin strips. Heat 2 more teaspoons of the peanut oil in wok; repeat process with remaining egg mixture.

5 Combine garlic, chillies, sugar, sauces and vinegar in small bowl; pour half the chilli mixture into small jug, reserve.

6 Combine pork in bowl with remaining chilli mixture. Heat remaining peanut oil in wok; stir-fry pork mixture until cooked through. Add prawns; stir-fry 1 minute. Add tofu; stir-fry, tossing gently to combine.

7 Remove wok from heat; add reserved chilli mixture, half the onion and vermicelli, toss gently. Sprinkle with remaining onion, omelette strips and coriander leaves.

serves 4
preparation time 35 minutes
cooking time 20 minutes
nutritional count per serving 22.3g total fat (4.7g saturated fat); 1898kJ (454 cal); 30.9g carbohydrate; 31.3g protein; 2.2g fibre

sticky pork with vegies

1 tablespoon honey
2 tablespoons light soy sauce
2 tablespoons brown sugar
1 teaspoon five-spice powder
1 teaspoon hot chilli powder
3 cloves garlic, crushed
1 teaspoon sesame oil
750g pork neck, cut into 3cm cubes
2 tablespoons peanut oil
½ cup (70g) unsalted peanuts, chopped coarsely
1 medium carrot (120g), cut into matchsticks
150g snow peas, trimmed, sliced thinly lengthways
2 tablespoons orange juice
3 kaffir lime leaves, shredded finely
4 green onions, sliced thinly

1 Combine honey, sauce, sugar, five-spice, chilli, garlic and sesame oil in large bowl; add pork, turn to coat in marinade. Cover; refrigerate 3 hours or overnight.
2 Heat half the peanut oil in wok; stir-fry nuts until browned. Drain.
3 Heat remaining oil in wok, add pork; stir-fry, in batches, until browned. Return pork to wok with carrot; stir-fry until pork is cooked.
4 Add snow peas, juice and lime leaves; stir-fry until snow peas are tender. Remove from heat; toss in onion and nuts.

serves 4
preparation time 15 minutes (plus refrigeration time)
cooking time 25 minutes
nutritional count per serving 33.7g total fat (8.1g saturated fat); 2366kJ (566 cal); 18.5g carbohydrate; 46.4g protein; 3.8g fibre

stir-fried pork
with buk choy and rice noodles

¼ cup (60ml) oyster sauce
2 tablespoons light soy sauce
2 tablespoons sweet sherry
1 tablespoon brown sugar
1 clove garlic, crushed
1 star anise, crushed
pinch five-spice powder
400g fresh rice noodles
2 teaspoons sesame oil
600g pork fillets, sliced thinly
700g baby buk choy, chopped coarsely

1 Combine sauces, sherry, sugar, garlic, star anise and five-spice in small jug.
2 Place noodles in large heatproof bowl, cover with boiling water; separate with fork, drain.
3 Heat oil in wok; stir-fry pork, in batches, until cooked.
4 Return pork to wok with sauce mixture, noodles and buk choy; stir-fry until buk choy is wilted.

serves 4
preparation time 10 minutes
cooking time 10 minutes
nutritional count per serving 6.7g total fat (1.6g saturated fat); 1492kJ (357 cal); 31.6g carbohydrate; 37.9g protein; 2.9g fibre

pork kway teow

400g fresh wide rice noodles
1 tablespoon peanut oil
600g pork mince
1 medium brown onion (150g), sliced thinly
1 medium red capsicum (200g), sliced thinly
10cm stick fresh lemon grass (20g), chopped finely
2 tablespoons light soy sauce
¼ cup (60ml) lemon juice
1 tablespoon grated palm sugar
2 fresh small red thai chillies, chopped finely
1 cup coarsely chopped fresh coriander

1 Place noodles in large heatproof bowl, cover with boiling water; separate noodles with fork, drain.
2 Heat half the oil in wok; stir-fry pork until cooked through. Remove from wok.
3 Heat remaining oil in wok; stir-fry onion, capsicum and lemon grass until onion softens.
4 Return pork to wok with noodles and combined sauce, juice and sugar; stir-fry until heated through. Remove from heat; stir in chilli and coriander.

serves 4
preparation time 20 minutes
cooking time 10 minutes
nutritional count per serving 15.6g total fat (4.7g saturated fat); 1660kJ (397 cal); 29g carbohydrate; 33.9g protein; 1.5g fibre

mixed green vegetables and fried tofu

You need to buy two bunches each of asparagus and broccolini for this recipe.

300g fresh firm silken tofu
1 tablespoon peanut oil
1 medium brown onion (150g),
    sliced thinly
2 cloves garlic, crushed
2cm piece fresh ginger (10g),
    grated
1 fresh small red thai chilli,
    chopped finely
340g asparagus, cut into
    3cm lengths
350g broccolini, cut into
    3cm lengths
200g sugar snap peas,
    trimmed
500g buk choy,
    chopped coarsely
¼ cup (60ml) vegetable stock
¼ cup (60ml) hoisin sauce
¼ cup (60ml) vegetarian
    mushroom oyster sauce
1 tablespoon lime juice
100g bean sprouts

1 Cut tofu into 2cm cubes; spread, in single layer, on absorbent-paper-lined tray. Cover tofu with more absorbent paper, stand 10 minutes.
2 Heat half the oil in wok; stir-fry tofu, in batches, until browned lightly.
3 Heat remaining oil in wok; stir-fry onion, garlic, ginger and chilli until onion softens. Add asparagus, broccolini and peas; stir-fry until vegetables are tender. Add buk choy, stock, sauces and juice; stir-fry until buk choy wilts.
4 Return tofu to wok; stir-fry until combined. Remove from heat; stir in sprouts.

serves 4
preparation time 25 minutes
cooking time 10 minutes
nutritional count per serving 11.6g total fat (1.8g saturated fat); 1191kJ (285 cal); 18.4g carbohydrate; 20.5g protein; 12.3g fibre

stir-fried asian greens in black bean sauce

2 cups (400g) jasmine rice
1 tablespoon peanut oil
150g sugar snap peas, trimmed
400g gai lan, chopped coarsely
200g snake beans, trimmed, cut into 5cm lengths
2 cloves garlic, sliced thinly
1 fresh small red thai chilli, chopped finely
2 medium zucchini (240g), sliced thickly
2 tablespoons black bean sauce
1 tablespoon kecap manis
1 teaspoon sesame oil
⅓ cup (50g) roasted unsalted cashews, chopped coarsely

1 Cook rice in large saucepan of boiling water, uncovered, until just tender; drain.
2 Meanwhile, heat peanut oil in wok; stir-fry peas, gai lan stems, beans, garlic, chilli and zucchini until stems are just tender.
3 Add sauce, kecap manis, sesame oil, gai lan leaves and nuts; stir-fry until leaves are just wilted.
4 Serve stir-fry with rice.

serves 4
preparation time 10 minutes
cooking time 15 minutes
nutritional count per serving 13.3g total fat (2.6g saturated fat); 2274kJ (544 cal); 89.5g carbohydrate; 15.4g protein; 8.8g fibre

stir-fried sweet and sour vegetables

2 cloves garlic
2 fresh small red thai chillies
500g asparagus
2 lebanese cucumbers (260g)
1 tablespoon peanut oil
100g snow peas
250g broccoli florets
1 medium green capsicum (200g), chopped coarsely
1 tablespoon light soy sauce
1 tablespoon white vinegar
1 tablespoon brown sugar

1 Cut garlic and chillies into thin strips. Cut asparagus into 5cm lengths; cut cucumbers in half lengthways, remove seeds, then slice thickly.
2 Heat oil in wok; stir-fry garlic and chilli until browned lightly, remove from wok.
3 Reheat oil in wok, add vegetables; stir-fry until vegetables are just tender.
4 Add combined sauce, vinegar and sugar; stir-fry 1 minute. Serve vegetables sprinkled with garlic and chillies.

serves 6
preparation time 20 minutes
cooking time 10 minutes
nutritional count per serving 3.4g total fat (0.6g saturated fat); 368kJ (88 cal); 6.3g carbohydrate; 5.8g protein; 4.4g fibre

nasi goreng

You need to cook 2 cups of jasmine rice the day before you want to make this, or any, fried rice recipe. Spread the rice in a thin layer on a tray, cover, and refrigerate overnight.

1 small brown onion (80g),
    chopped coarsely
2 cloves garlic, quartered
5cm piece fresh ginger (25g),
    chopped coarsely
2 fresh long red chillies,
    chopped coarsely
1 tablespoon peanut oil
4 eggs, beaten lightly
150g oyster mushrooms,
    chopped coarsely
1 medium green capsicum
    (200g), chopped coarsely
1 medium red capsicum
    (200g), chopped coarsely
200g baby corn, chopped
    coarsely
4 cups cooked jasmine rice
1 cup (80g) bean sprouts
3 green onions, sliced thinly
2 tablespoons japanese
    soy sauce
1 tablespoon kecap manis

1 Blend or process brown onion, garlic, ginger and chilli until almost smooth.
2 Heat 1 teaspoon of the oil in wok; add half the egg, swirl wok to make a thin omelette. Cook, uncovered, until egg is just set. Remove from wok; cut into thick strips. Repeat process with another 1 teaspoon of the oil and remaining egg.
3 Heat remaining oil in wok; stir-fry onion mixture until fragrant. Add mushrooms, capsicums and corn; stir-fry until tender.
4 Add rice, sprouts, green onion, sauce and kecap manis; stir-fry until heated through.
5 Serve nasi goreng topped with omelette.

serves 4
preparation time 20 minutes
cooking time 15 minutes
nutritional count per serving 11.2g total fat (2.5g saturated fat); 1843kJ (441 cal); 66.8g carbohydrate; 17.6g protein; 7.2g fibre

pad thai

200g dried rice stick noodles
2 cloves garlic, quartered
2 fresh small red thai chillies, chopped coarsely
2 tablespoons peanut oil
2 eggs, beaten lightly
1 cup (80g) fried shallots
125g packet fried tofu, cut into 2cm cubes
¼ cup (35g) roasted unsalted peanuts, chopped coarsely
3 cups (240g) bean sprouts
6 green onions, sliced thinly
2 tablespoons light soy sauce
1 tablespoon lime juice
2 tablespoons coarsely chopped fresh coriander

1   Place noodles in large heatproof bowl, cover with boiling water; stand until just tender, drain.
2   Meanwhile, using mortar and pestle, crush garlic and chilli to a paste.
3   Heat 2 teaspoons of the oil in wok; add egg, swirl wok to form thin omelette. Cook omelette over medium heat until almost set. Remove omelette from wok; roll tightly then slice thinly.
4   Heat remaining oil in wok; stir-fry garlic paste and shallots until fragrant. Add tofu; stir-fry 1 minute. Add half the nuts, half the sprouts and half the onion; stir-fry until spouts are just wilted.
5   Add noodles, sauce and juice; stir-fry until hot. Remove from heat; sprinkle omelette, coriander and remaining nuts, sprouts and onion over pad thai.

serves 4
preparation time 20 minutes
cooking time 10 minutes
nutritional count per serving 19.6g total fat (3.4g saturated fat); 1246kJ (298 cal); 15.1g carbohydrate; 13.4g protein; 4.3g fibre

glossary

bamboo shoots the tender pale-yellow edible shoots of the bamboo plant, available in cans; must be rinsed and drained before use.

broccolini a cross between broccoli and chinese kale; milder and sweeter than broccoli. Each long stem is topped by a loose floret that closely resembles broccoli; from floret to stem, broccolini is completely edible.

buk choy also known as bok choy, pak choi, chinese white cabbage or chinese chard; has a fresh, mild mustard taste. Baby buk choy, also known as pak kat farang or shanghai bok choy, is much smaller and more tender.

capsicum also known as bell pepper or, simply, pepper. Discard seeds and membranes before use.

chilli available in many types and sizes. Use rubber gloves when seeding and chopping fresh chillies as they can burn your skin. Removing seeds and membranes lessens the heat level.
red thai small, hot, and bright red in colour.

chinese cooking wine also known as hao hsing or chinese rice wine; made from fermented rice, wheat, sugar and salt. Available from Asian food stores. Mirin or sherry can be substituted.

dried shrimp (goong hang) salted, sun-dried prawns ranging in size from not much larger than a rice seed to about 1cm in length. They are sold packaged in all Asian grocery stores.

eggplant also known as aubergine.

five-spice powder also known as chinese five-spice; a fragrant mixture of ground cinnamon, cloves, star anise, sichuan pepper and fennel seeds.

flour plain an all-purpose flour made from wheat.

gai lan also known as chinese broccoli, gai larn, kanah, gai lum and chinese kale; appreciated more for its stems than its coarse leaves.

ginger also known as green or root ginger; the thick root of a tropical plant.

kaffir lime leaves also known as bai magrood; look like two glossy dark green leaves joined end to end, forming a rounded hourglass shape. A strip of fresh lime peel may be substituted for each kaffir lime leaf.

kecap manis also known as ketjap manis; a thick soy sauce with added sugar and spices.

lebanese cucumber short, slender and thin-skinned. Has a tender, edible skin, tiny, yielding seeds and a sweet, fresh taste.

lemon grass a tall, clumping, lemon-smelling and tasting, sharp-edged grass; the white lower part of the stem is used, finely chopped.

mince also known as ground meat.

mirin a champagne-coloured Japanese cooking wine; made of glutinous rice and alcohol and used expressly for cooking. Should not be confused with sake.

mushrooms
oyster also known as abalone; grey-white mushroom shaped like a fan. Prized for their smooth texture and subtle, oyster-like flavour.
shiitake when fresh are also known as chinese black, forest or golden oak; are large and meaty. When dried, they are known as donko or dried chinese mushrooms; rehydrate before use.

noodles
dried rice stick also known as sen lek, ho fun or kway teow; come in different widths. Soak in hot water to soften.
fresh rice (also called khao pun ho fun, sen yau, pho or kway tiau, on the packet). Purchase in strands (either thin or wide) or large sheets, which are then cut into the desired noodle size.They do not need to be pre-cooked before use.

hokkien also known as stir-fry noodles; fresh wheat noodles resembling thick, yellow-brown spaghetti. Soak in hot water before use to separate strands.

rice vermicelli also known as sen mee, mei fun or bee hoon. Soak in hot water until softened then boil briefly and rinse with hot water.

singapore pre-cooked wheat noodles best described as a thinner version of hokkien; soak in hot water before use.

thin fresh egg also known as ba mee or yellow noodles; made from wheat flour and eggs. Range in size from very fine strands to wide, spaghetti-like pieces as thick as a shoelace.

pepper medley a mixture of black, white, green and pink peppercorns, coriander seeds and allspice; sold in grinders in supermarkets.

sambal oelek (also ulek or olek) Indonesian in origin; a salty paste made from ground chillies and vinegar.

sauces

black bean a Chinese sauce made from fermented soy beans, spices, water and wheat flour.

char siu a Chinese sauce made from sugar, water, salt, fermented soy bean paste, honey, soy sauce, malt syrup and spices. Found at supermarkets.

chilli we use a hot Chinese variety made from red thai chillies, salt and vinegar. Use sparingly, increasing the quantity to suit your taste.

fish also called nam pla or nuoc nam; made from pulverised salted fermented fish, most often anchovies. Has a pungent smell and strong taste, so use sparingly.

hoisin a thick, sweet and spicy Chinese paste made from salted fermented soy beans, onions and garlic.

soy made from fermented soy beans. Several variations are available in supermarkets and Asian food stores. *Dark soy* is deep brown, almost black in colour; rich, with a thicker consistency than other types. Pungent but not particularly salty. *Japanese soy* is possibly the best low-sodium table soy and the one to choose if you only want one variety. *Light soy* is pale, thin and the saltiest tasting; used in dishes in which the natural colour of the ingredients is to be maintained. Not to be confused with salt-reduced or low-sodium soy sauces.

oyster a rich, brown sauce made from oysters and their brine, cooked with salt and soy sauce, and thickened with starches.

sweet chilli a mild sauce made from red chillies, sugar, garlic and vinegar.

teriyaki made from soy sauce, mirin, sugar, ginger and other spices.

vegetarian mushroom oyster this is a "vegetarian" oyster sauce available made from blended mushrooms and soy sauce.

sichuan peppercorns small, red-brown aromatic seeds having a peppery-lemon flavour.

snake beans long (about 40cm), thin, round fresh green beans. Also called yard-long beans because of their length.

palm sugar also known as nam tan pip, jaggery, jawa or gula melaka; made from the sap of the sugar palm tree. Light brown to black in colour and usually sold in rock-hard cakes. Can be substituted with brown sugar.

thai basil also known as horapa; has small leaves, purplish stems and a slight aniseed taste.

vinegar, rice a colourless vinegar made from fermented rice and flavoured with sugar and salt. Also known as seasoned rice vinegar; sherry can be substituted.

wombok also known as peking cabbage, chinese cabbage or petsai. Elongated in shape with pale green, crinkly leaves.

zucchini also known as courgette.

conversion chart

MEASURES

One Australian metric measuring cup holds approximately 250ml, one Australian metric tablespoon holds 20ml, one Australian metric teaspoon holds 5ml.

The difference between one country's measuring cups and another's is within a 2- or 3-teaspoon variance, and will not affect your cooking results. North America, New Zealand and the United Kingdom use a 15ml tablespoon. All cup and spoon measurements are level. The most accurate way of measuring dry ingredients is to weigh them. When measuring liquids, use a clear glass or plastic jug with metric markings.

We use large eggs with an average weight of 60g.

DRY MEASURES

METRIC	IMPERIAL
15g	½oz
30g	1oz
60g	2oz
90g	3oz
125g	4oz (¼lb)
155g	5oz
185g	6oz
220g	7oz
250g	8oz (½lb)
280g	9oz
315g	10oz
345g	11oz
375g	12oz (¾lb)
410g	13oz
440g	14oz
470g	15oz
500g	16oz (1lb)
750g	24oz (1½lb)
1kg	32oz (2lb)

LIQUID MEASURES

METRIC	IMPERIAL
30ml	1 fluid oz
60ml	2 fluid oz
100ml	3 fluid oz
125ml	4 fluid oz
150ml	5 fluid oz (¼ pint/1 gill)
190ml	6 fluid oz
250ml	8 fluid oz
300ml	10 fluid oz (½ pint)
500ml	16 fluid oz
600ml	20 fluid oz (1 pint)
1000ml (1 litre)	1¾ pints

LENGTH MEASURES

METRIC	IMPERIAL
3mm	⅛in
6mm	¼in
1cm	½in
2cm	¾in
2.5cm	1in
5cm	2in
6cm	2½in
8cm	3in
10cm	4in
13cm	5in
15cm	6in
18cm	7in
20cm	8in
23cm	9in
25cm	10in
28cm	11in
30cm	12in (1ft)

OVEN TEMPERATURES

These oven temperatures are only a guide for conventional ovens. For fan-forced ovens, check the manufacturer's manual.

	°C (CELSIUS)	°F (FAHRENHEIT)	GAS MARK
Very slow	120	250	½
Slow	150	275 – 300	1 – 2
Moderately slow	160	325	3
Moderate	180	350 – 375	4 – 5
Moderately hot	200	400	6
Hot	220	425 – 450	7 – 8
Very hot	240	475	9

index

A
asian greens in black bean
  sauce, stir-fried 52

B
beef
  chow mein 28
  ginger teriyaki 23
  hokkien mee with 27
  in satay sauce 24
  with oyster sauce 20

C
char siu lamb and
  noodle stir-fry 36
chicken
  and pork sang choy bow 40
  and thai basil stir-fry 11
  fried rice 15
chilli crab 3
chow mein, beef 28
crab, chilli 3
crisp twice-fried lamb
  with thai basil 35
cucumber salad 8

D
dressing, larb 32

F
fried rice, chicken 15

G
ginger teriyaki beef 23

H
hokkien mee with beef 27
honey and five-spice lamb
  with buk choy 39

K
kung pao prawns 7

L
lamb
  and noodle stir-fry,
    char siu 36
  crisp twice-fried, with
    thai basil 35
  honey and five-spice,
    with buk choy 39
  larb 32
  mongolian, stir-fry 31
larb dressing 32
larb lamb 32

M
mee goreng 19
mee krob 43
mixed green vegetables
  and fried tofu 51
mongolian lamb stir-fry 31

N
nasi goreng 56
noodle and char siu
  lamb stir-fry 36
noodles, rice, and buk choy
  with stir-fried pork 47
noodles, singapore 16

P
pad sieu 12
pad thai 59
pork
  and chicken
    sang choy bow 40
  kway teow 48
  with buk choy and
    rice noodles, stir-fried 47
  sticky, with vegies 44
prawns, kung pao 7

R
rice, chicken fried 15

S
salad, cucumber 8
salt and pepper squid with
  cucumber salad 8
sang choy bow, pork
  and chicken 40
satay sauce, beef in 24
seafood
  chilli crab 4
  kung pao prawns 7
  salt and pepper squid
    with cucumber salad 8
singapore noodles 16
squid, salt and pepper,
  with cucumber salad 8
sticky pork with vegies 44
sweet and sour vegetables,
  stir-fried 55

T
teriyaki ginger beef 23
tofu, fried, and mixed
  green vegetables 51
twice-fried lamb, crisp,
  with thai basil 35

V
vegetarian
  mixed green vegetables
    and fried tofu 51
  nasi goreng 56
  pad thai 59
  stir-fried asian greens in
    black bean sauce 52
  stir-fried sweet and sour
    vegetables 55

Are you missing some of the world's favourite cookbooks?

The Australian Women's Weekly cookbooks are available from bookshops, cookshops, supermarkets and other stores all over the world. You can also buy direct from the publisher, using the order form below.

MINI SERIES £3.50 190x138MM 64 PAGES

TITLE	QTY	TITLE	QTY	TITLE	QTY
4 Fast Ingredients		Easy Pies & Pastries		Pasta	
15-minute Feasts		Finger Food		Potatoes	
50 Fast Chicken Fillets		Fishcakes & Crispybakes		Roast	
50 Fast Desserts		Gluten-free Cooking		Salads	
After-work Stir-fries		Grills & Barbecues		Simple Slices	
Barbecue Chicken		Healthy Everyday Food 4 Kids		Simply Seafood	
Bites		Ice-creams & Sorbets		Skinny Food	
Bowl Food		Indian Cooking		Spanish Favourites	
Burgers, Rösti & Fritters		Italian Favourites		Stir-fries	
Cafe Cakes		Jams & Jellies		Stir-fry Favourites	
Cafe Food		Japanese Favourites		Summer Salads	
Casseroles		Kebabs & Skewers		Tagines & Couscous	
Casseroles & Curries		Kids Party Food		Tapas, Antipasto & Mezze	
Char-grills & Barbecues		Last-minute Meals		Tarts	
Cheesecakes, Pavlova & Trifles		Lebanese Cooking		Tex-Mex	
Chinese Favourites		Low-Fat Delicious		Thai Favourites	
Christmas Cakes & Puddings		Malaysian Favourites		The Fast Egg	
Christmas Favourites		Mince		Vegetarian	
Cocktails		Mince Favourites		Vegie Main Meals	
Crumbles & Bakes		Muffins		Vietnamese Favourites	
Cupcakes & Cookies		Noodles		Wok	
Curries		Noodles & Stir-fries			
Dips & Dippers		Outdoor Eating			
Dried Fruit & Nuts		Party Food			
Drinks		Pickles and Chutneys		TOTAL COST £	

Photocopy and complete coupon below

Name _____

Address _____

_____ Postcode _____

Country _____ Phone (business hours) _____

Email*(optional) _____
* *By including your email address, you consent to receipt of any email regarding this magazine, and other emails which inform you of ACP's other publications, products, services and events, and to promote third party goods and services you may be interested in.*

I enclose my cheque/money order for £ _____ or please charge £ _____
to my: ☐ Access ☐ Mastercard ☐ Visa ☐ Diners Club

Card number | | | | | | | | | | | | | | | | |

3 digit security code *(found on reverse of card)* _____

Cardholder's
signature _____ Expiry date ___ /___

To order: Mail or fax – photocopy or complete the order form above, send your credit card details or cheque payable to: Australian Consolidated Press (UK), 10 Scirocco Close, Moulton Park Office Village, Northampton NN3 6AP, phone (+44) (01) 604 642200, fax (+44) (01) 604 642300, e-mail books@acpuk.com or order online at www.acpuk.com
Non-UK residents: We accept the credit cards listed on the coupon, or cheques, drafts or International Money Orders payable in sterling and drawn on a UK bank. Credit card charges are at the exchange rate current at the time of payment.
All pricing current at time of going to press and subject to change/availability.
Postage and packing UK: Add £1.00 per order plus 75p per book.
Postage and packing overseas: Add £2.00 per order plus £1.50 per book. **Offer ends 31.12.2008**